THE LAST DAYS OF STEAM IN
NORTHAMPTONSHIRE

THE LAST DAYS OF STEAM IN
NORTHAMPTONSHIRE

JOHN M.C. HEALY

ALAN SUTTON

ALAN SUTTON PUBLISHING LIMITED
BRUNSWICK ROAD · GLOUCESTER · UK

ALAN SUTTON PUBLISHING INC.
WOLFEBORO FALLS · NH · USA

First published in the United Kingdom 1989
First published in the United States of America 1990

British Library Cataloguing in Publication Data
Healy, John
Last days of steam in Northamptonshire.
1. Northamptonshire. Steam locomotives, history.
I. Title
625.2'61'094255
ISBN 0-86299-613-9

Library of Congress Cataloging in Publication Data applied for

Front Cover: 2P class No. 40646 leads No. 40026 through Northampton Bridge Street with an SLS special on a lovely day in April 1962 – Colour Rail

Back Cover: In January 1961 in deep snow class 6MT No. 44691 pauses at Piddington signal-box on the Bedford line with a short freight – Colour Rail

Typesetting and origination by
Alan Sutton Publishing Limited
Printed in the United Kingdom by
Dotesios Printers Limited

Introduction

Like many other counties in England, Scotland and Wales, Northamptonshire in the late nineteenth century became an area ripe for exploitation by up-and-coming railway companies who saw an opportunity to offer a transport system that would be better than the existing roads, canals and rivers, which were unable to afford access to the important centres and villages within the county.

The general idea was to build railways to enable passengers to travel over wider distances, and, by linking communities with other towns and villages, to open up new markets for local produce. In addition, the railways created employment, both in their construction and in their operation. This had rather a dramatic effect as rural occupations became short of labour due to the attractive wages offered by the railways.

Such was the success of the railways that many schemes were put before parliament to build lines in Northamptonshire which never materialised. In fact, Railway Mania hit the county in a big way and by the time the last line was completed, some seventy-six stations existed.

Northamptonshire had four different categories of lines within its boundaries, namely main, cross-country, branch and industrial complexes. The three main lines all emanated from London, running to the East Midlands, to the North West and Scotland and to the East Midlands, North West and Scotland respectively, while the numerous cross-country routes linked the three together. With these and the various branch lines and the spurs into ironstone quarries, it was possible to see not only a variety of passenger and freight workings but also a fine selection of motive power. One delight for enthusiasts of the time was that Northamptonshire boasted four motive power depots, at Kettering, Wellingborough, Northampton and Woodford Halse.

Sadly, all these features and many lines, including the former Great Central route that was once part of an ambitious plan to link Manchester and Paris, have disappeared, mainly as a result of Dr Beeching's re-shaping of British Railways in the mid to late 1960s. It is a disquieting thought that, of the original seventy-six stations and four locomotive depots, only five stations are still open in Northamptonshire today.

John M.C. Healy

THE LAST DAYS OF STEAM IN
NORTHAMPTONSHIRE

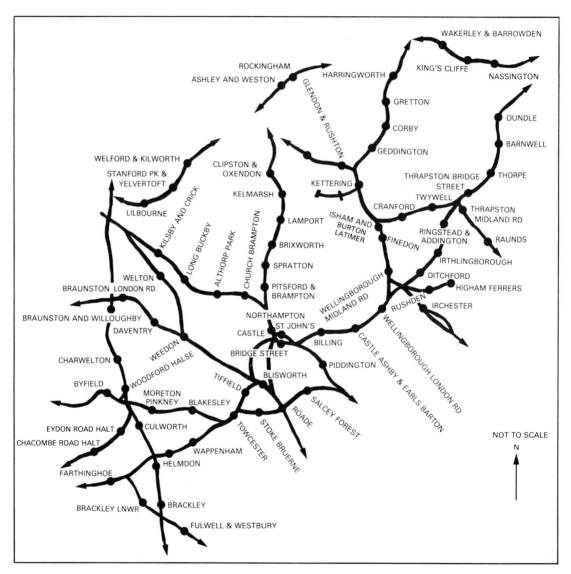

LAST DAYS OF STEAM IN NORTHAMPTONSHIRE
Only locations relevant to the text are shown.

The Great Central Route

Class 5 No. 44872 stands in the up main line platform of Brackley Central with a heavily laden 8.15 a.m. ex-Nottingham Victoria train which is attracting much attention as it is the last day of working on the old Great Central main line.

K.C.H. Fairey

Passing the now lifted cross-over and goods yard south of Brackley Central, a diesel multiple unit heads the 12.38 p.m. ex-London Marylebone towards the town's station on its journey to Nottingham Victoria on the last day of passenger services.

K.C.H. Fairey

A bleak view of Brackley Central with snow still present in this March 1963 photograph. On the left and right respectively are the main booking hall and station house, while in the centre lie the platform buildings.

D. Thompson

A three-quarter view of a rather clean looking B1 class engine No. 61106 seen waiting under the footbridge at Brackley Central with a departure for Nottingham Victoria on 24 July 1961.

F.G. Cockman

Brackley Central from the north end, showing the whole station complex at a rather busy moment on 24 March 1961. In the background a local pick-up freight for Aylesbury has just left the goods yard and is crossing the viaduct along from the signal cabin and water tower, while nearest the camera a train of empty stock is stabled in the siding and a B1 class No. 61186 waits to head off to Helmdon, Culworth and Woodford Halse with a local working.

B. Brooksbank

The immaculately kept island platform at Helmdon in the late 1950s showing the toilet block, waiting rooms and ticket office from the down main line side.

Author's Collection

Helmdon for Sulgrave station looking south towards Brackley Central showing the economic design of these ex-Great Central country platforms.

D. Thompson

One of the ex-War Department engines purchased from the Ministry of Supply by British Railways in 1948, No. 90046 heads towards Culworth with a train of mineral empties on a Woodford Halse to Annesley 'Runner' working on 15 April 1952.

Les Hanson

A sad day for the viaduct at Helmdon as it has shuddered for the last time with the passage of a train. The magnificent nine-arched structure was built to cross the River Tove and the Northampton and Banbury Junction Railway, which also had a station at Helmdon until it closed in 1951.

Author's Collection

Culworth station showing the main station buildings and signal cabin on a dull day in May 1961. The goods yard lay on the right, though by the time this picture was taken the station had been closed for some three years.

D. Thompson

Built of Northamptonshire stone, the white-walled and black-timbered Woodford Halse Social Club was a popular meeting place for railway workers until the closure of the former Great Central main line in 1966. The building had been acquired by British Railways for use as a social club in 1955.

Author's Collection

The stairway which led up to the main platform at Woodford Halse station in 1962. Note the new-looking Standard Vanguard Estate to the right of the picture.

Author's Collection

Woodford Halse on 3 September 1966 showing the 5.15 p.m. ex-Nottingham Victoria service, about to form the last ever daytime departure on the former Great Central main line. For Woodford, bidding farewell to the railway was a double blow as it removed the main source of employment from the village.

K.C.H. Fairey

Woodford Halse locomotive depot in happier times on 7 May 1961 showing British Railways 9F class heavy freight engine No. 92215. Sometimes these engines were employed on relief passenger workings.

K.C.H. Fairey

Woodford Halse locomotive depot in the prime of its life on 15 March 1953 showing a tremendous number of engines present. At the front of the line-up on the left is an ex-Great Central J11 class 3F 0-6-0 No. 64388.

B.W. Brooksbank

Woodford Halse locomotive depot on 3 October 1964 showing J39 class 0-6-0 No. 64747 at rest by the water tank. In the background are the pumping house and the mechanical coaling plant, underneath which are a number of internal coal-supply wagons.

K.C.H. Fairey

Withdrawn but not quite life-expired, ex-London and North Eastern Railway J39 class No. 64742 stands in use as a stationary boiler at the rear of Woodford Halse locomotive depot on 7 May 1961.
K.C.H. Fairey

Super-power at Woodford Halse as 'Prince Coronation' class No. 46251 *City of Nottingham* waits at the up main line platform with the RCTS 'East Midlander' rail tour on 9 May 1964.
K.C.H. Fairey

Charwelton station on a rather crisp day just three days before local services ceased to call here. The station did more trade in goods traffic, as the yard was connected to a siding into a local ironstone mine.

D. Thompson

On 29 July 1950, 01 class No. 63806 slowly skirts round the island platform at Charwelton station with a mixed freight train for York.

Les Hanson

B1 class No. 61111 draws away from Charwelton on 29 July 1950 with a very mixed selection of coaches forming an evening Aylesbury to Nottingham all stations service.

Les Hanson

An immaculate ex-London and North Eastern Railway B1 class No. 61083 rounds the platform at Charwelton with ease as it rushes along with a Marylebone to Manchester working.

K.C.H. Fairey

On the same day a B1 class No. 61186, in early British Railways livery, draws effortlessly past the island platform at Charwelton with an Aylesbury to Nottingham 'ord' (an ordinary working calling at all stations).

Les Hanson

With a fine head of steam L1 class No. 67789 heads away from Charwelton station on 22 March 1962 with a local Aylesbury Town to Rugby Central service.

K.C.H. Fairey

Having just cleared Charwelton station complex, 01 class No. 63806 heads off towards Catesby Tunnel with a Swindon to York freight train on 27 July 1950.

Les Hanson

On a misty day in March 1962 a 9F class heavy freight locomotive No. 92094 pulls away from Catesby Tunnel with a laden mixed freight train for Woodford Halse, where the wagons will be sorted and despatched to their respective destinations.

K.C.H. Fairey

Near Staverton Road between Charwelton, and Braunston and Willoughby, class 9F No. 92030, one of the mainstays of motive power on freight workings after 1955 on the old Great Central, heads south with an up mixed goods.

K.C.H. Fairey

Another 9F class, No. 92076, just south of Braunston and Willoughby, steams along the embankment near the border between Northamptonshire and Warwickshire with an up Annesley to Woodford Halse 'Windcutter' freight on 24 May 1958.

Author's Collection

'Jubilee' class No. 45565 heads the 12.25 ex-Nottingham Victoria to London Marylebone semi-fast service southwards near Braunston and Willoughby station on 8 July 1961.

Mike Mitchell

The site of Eydon Road Halt and signal cabin on the Woodford Halse to Banbury link line which joined the old Great Central to the Great Western main line.

D. Thompson

On 5 August 1950, V2 class No. 60877 heads a fully laden cross-country Newcastle to Bournemouth express passenger train towards Banbury near Eydon Road.

Les Hanson

Between Eydon Road and Chacombe Road B16 class No. 61434 heads a train of empty articulated carriage stock back to Woodford Halse on 5 August 1950.

Les Hanson

Chacombe Road signal cabin in 1957 and the site of the Halt, which had closed a year and three months before. The Halt lay between the signal and hut in the background.

D. Thompson

The Banbury to Verney Junction and Northampton Lines

A pencil sketch of the signal-box at Cockley Brake Junction, the point where the lines to Towcester and Verney Junction branched off from the Banbury Merton Street line.

P. Slater

BANBURY — BLETCHLEY														

BRITISH RAILWAYS (L.M.R.)   TABLE **6**

WEEKDAYS ONLY

	a.m.	a.m.	a.m.	p.m.	p.m.	p.m.	SX a.m.	SO p.m.	p.m.	p.m.	SX p.m.	SO p.m.	SO a.m.	SO p.m.
Banbury (Merton St.)	5 48	9 14		11 5	1 45		3 45			5 45		7 22	7 22	9 48	1052
Brackley	7 3	9 30		1120	2 0		4 0			6 0		7 37	7 37	10 2	11 7
Fulwell and Westbury	7 8	9 35		1125	2 5		4 5			6 5		7 43	7 43	10 8	1112
Water Stratford Halt	7 12	9 39		1129	2 9		4 9			6 9		7 46	7 46	1011	1116
Radclive Halt	7 16	9 43		1133	213		413			613		7 50	7 50	1015	1120
Buckingham {a	7 19	9 46		1136	216		416			616		7 54	7 54	1019	1123
{d	7 20		9 55	1137		2 35		436	436		636	7 55	7 55		1124
Padbury	7 24		9 59	1141		2 39		440	440		640	8 0	8 0		1128
Verney Junction {a	7 29			1146							646	8 4	8 4		1134
{d	7 30		10 4	1147		2 44		445	445		647	8 5	8 5		1135
Winslow	7 34		10 10	1151		2 50		451	451		652	8 9	8 9		1140
Swanbourne	7 38		10 15	1155		2 55		456	456		657	8 14	8 14		1144
Bletchley	7 47		10 25	12 4		3 5		5 6	5 6		7 7	8 23	8 23		1153
Cambridge ...... a	1131			11 48		5 25			815			9 57	9 59		
Northampton Cas. a	8D25		1254	11 23		4K43		6 8	731			8 29	12 9	9 25	1 26

	a.m.	SO a.m.	SX a.m.	a.m.	a.m.	SX a.m.	SO a.m.	p.m.	a.m.	p.m.	p.m.	SO p.m.	SO p.m.	p.m.
Northampton Cas. d	4 21	635	650	8 0		10 0		1249		243		415	752	
Cambridge d						9 23	9 38	1126	1126			2 5	618	
Bletchley	5 18	755	755	9 10		1230	1230	1 55	1 55	335		528	831	850
Swanbourne		8 4	8 4	9 20		1239	1239	2 5	2 5	345		538	845	
Winslow		8 8	8 8	9 25		1243	1243	2 10	2 10	350		544	850	
Verney Junction {a		812	812	9 30		1247	1247	2 15	2 15	355		549	855	9 3
{d		813	813	9 31		1248	1248	2 16	2 16	356		550		9 4
Padbury		817	817	9 35		1252	1252	2 20	2 20	4 0		554		9 8
Buckingham {a	5 38	822	822	9 41		1256	1256	2 26	2 26	4 6		6 0		913
{d	5 47	625	825		9 52	1257	1257	2 30	2 30		430	630		914	1023
Radclive Halt		827	E27		9 54	1259	1259	2 32	2 32		432	632		916
Water Stratford Halt	5B51	831	831		9 58	1 3	1 3	2 36	2 36		436	636		920
Fulwell and Westbury	5 54	835	83		10 2	7 1	7 1	2 40	2 40		440	640		924
Brackley	6 4	841	841		10 8	1 13	1 13	2 46	2 46		446	646		929
Banbury (Merton St.)	6 19	856	856		1023	1 28	1 28	3 1	3 1		5 17	7 1		944	1048

B—Monday only.   D—8 52 on Sat.   K—4 25 on Sat.   SO or S—Saturday only.   SX—Not Saturday.

The 1958/9 timetable showing departure and arrival times for Fulwell and Westbury at the time of the introduction of the diesel railcar service between Banbury Merton Street and Buckingham.
Author's Collection

The main station building at Brackley on the former London and North Western Railway line on 30 April 1966, two years after the last regular working passed through the station. The weed-ridden tracks in the foreground were finally lifted the following year, between February and April 1967.

H.C. Casserley

Brackley LNWR station looking towards Buckingham on 24 March 1961, two months after closure to passenger services. Goods services between Buckingham and Banbury Merton Street continued for a further two years. The depot on the left belonged to R. Fenwick and Co., who sold second-hand steam and diesel engines for industrial use.

B. Brooksbank

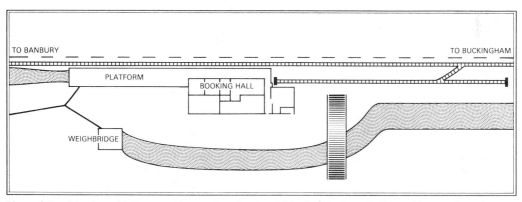

Plan of Farthinghoe Station on the ex-London and North Western Railway Verney Junction to Banbury branch, as it was just before closure on 29 November 1952.

Author's Collection

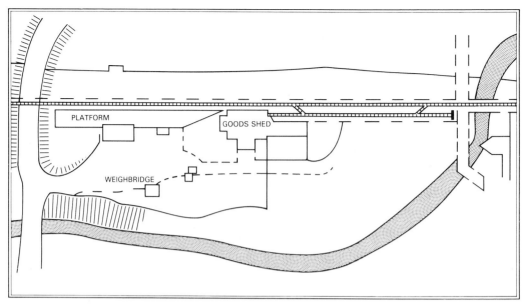

Track layout of Helmdon Village station in 1950; as can be seen from the large goods shed, it dealt with more of this kind of traffic than passengers.

Author's Collection

MOTOR CAR ACTS, 1896 AND 1903.

NOTICE.

THIS BRIDGE IS INSUFFICIENT TO CARRY A HEAVY MOTOR CAR THE REGISTERED AXLE WEIGHT OF ANY AXLE OF WHICH EXCEEDS THREE TONS, OR THE REGISTERED AXLE WEIGHTS OF THE SEVERAL AXLES OF WHICH EXCEED IN THE AGGREGATE FIVE TONS, OR A HEAVY MOTOR CAR DRAWING A TRAILER IF THE REGISTERED AXLE WEIGHTS OF THE SEVERAL AXLES OF THE HEAVY MOTOR CAR AND THE AXLE WEIGHTS OF THE SEVERAL AXLES OF THE TRAILER EXCEED IN THE AGGREGATE FIVE TONS.

EAST AND WEST JUNCTION, STRATFORD-ON-AVON, TOWCESTER AND MIDLAND JUNCTION RAILWAYS. STRATFORD-ON-AVON.

An old Stratford-upon-Avon and Midland Junction Railway (Northampton and Banbury Junction line) cast-iron motor-car weight restriction notice rescued from Wappenham station on 29 October 1951, the day of closure.

F.G. Cockman

The Shakespeare Route

On 31 May 1963, 8F 2-8-0 No. 48349 heads a couple of brake-vans to Byfield Ironstone Company's sidings through Byfield station, which had closed to passengers some eleven years earlier in April 1952.

B. Brooksbank

The rather derelict-looking station at Byfield just before closure to all traffic in June 1965, facing Woodford Halse. Note the newish concrete sleepers through both platforms.

Lens of Sutton

Class 3F No. 43222 with a train of blood-and-custard liveried Gresley rolling stock stands at the Woodford Halse end of Byfield station in April 1956 with the 'Stratford-upon-Avon and Midland Junction Railway Farewell Rail Tour'.

Colour Rail

Byfield Ironstone Company's locomotive No. MW/1235 lies dormant on one of the ironstone quarry sidings on 16 June 1958.

R.M. Casserley

Locomotive No. MW193 being prepared for action on 16 June 1958 under the watchful eye of one of the photographers.

H.C. Casserley

Under steam, Byfield Ironstone Company locomotive No. MW/1235 heads along to Byfield, crossing the Upper Boddington, where a super vintage saloon car is parked.

R.M. Casserley

L1 class No. 67789 shunts a mixed freight train at Woodford West onto a couple of brake-vans sitting on the former Woodford South Chord which linked the Great Central line with the Shakespeare route. The line in the middle led to Northampton, while that on the left went as far as Woodford Halse station.

Author's Collection

MORTON PINKNEY

A drawing of the nameboard displayed on Moreton Pinkney signal cabin.

Author's Collection

Blakesley sation on the old Stratford-upon-Avon and Midland Junction Railway seen here in May 1951, a year before closure. Up until 1940 a miniature railway existed leading from the station yard to the nearby hall, which was rased to the ground in 1957.

Lens of Sutton

At Greens Norton Junction the old Stratford-upon-Avon and Midland Junction Railway and the Northampton and Banbury lines converged and ran into Towcester station, which is depicted in this overall view taken on 23 July 1957.

K.C.H. Fairey

A close-up view of 2P class No. 44076 as it draws a mixed freight from Northampton Castle through the deserted station at Towcester on 23 July 1957, four years after the last passenger trains between Stratford and Blisworth. Services to Banbury Merton Street had ceased as early as 2 July 1951.

K.C.H. Fairey

Having just got the right away from Towcester, 2P class No. 44317 slowly draws a mineral train for Fenny Compton and Stratford-upon-Avon past the very busy goods yard.

K.C.H. Fairey

The main station buildings at Stoke Bruerne on 12 November 1955 which are still in remarkably good order, considering that passengers ceased to use the station some four months after it opened on 31 March 1893. However, the single siding that the complex boasted still catered for goods traffic until 2 June 1952.

Les Hanson

2P Class No. 43971 draws past the derelict platform at Stoke Bruerne with a parcels train for Northampton Castle on 29 November 1955.

Les Hanson

The West Coast Main Line

With evidence of preparatory work for electrification in progress, 8P class No. 46228 *Duchess of Rutland* heads north through Roade towards Rugby with a parcels train on a wintry day in February 1963.

K.C.H. Fairey

2P class No. 43873 is seen trundling a freight working along the old Stratford-upon-Avon and Midland Junction Railway towards Stoke Bruerne. Just to the right of the engine on the lower level can be seen the main line to the north-west and Scotland.

K.C.H. Fairey

An aerial view of Roade Cutting showing the Northampton lines on the left and the route to Rugby on the right, along which 'Royal Scot' class No. 46156 *The South Wales Borderer* is heading a Euston to Glasgow working on 29 july 1950.

Les Hanson

On 3 June 1962 8P class 4-6-2 No. 46200 *The Princess Royal*, storms through Roade station with the 'Aberdeen Flyer' for London Euston.

K.C.H. Fairey

On the same day, this time at the north end of Roade Cutting, 'Jubilee' class No. 45733 *Novelty* is seen on an afternoon Manchester working.

Les Hanson

Blisworth London and North Western Railway station looking south towards Roade in 1955. In the platform on the far left of the picture a local train is just about to set off for Northampton Castle.
H.C. Casserley

The rather dilapidated station buildings at Blisworth on the former London and North Western Railway seen just after closure on 4 January 1960. Blisworth also had a further station to the left of the picture which served the line to Stratford-upon-Avon.

Les Hanson

An overall view of both stations at Blisworth, that of the London and North Western Railway on the left, and that of the Stratford-upon-Avon and Midland Junction Railway on the right. The former closed on 4 January 1960 while the latter ceased to function on 7 April 1952.

Lens of Sutton

Still in London Midland and Scottish Railway livery, a 2P class No. 3521 in a rather grimy condition heads a single-coach train away from Blisworth to Stratford-upon-Avon in 1950.

Les Hanson

46

Away with the old and up with the new as the former Weedon station encounters the last stages of demolition at about the same time as preparatory work is being effected in connection with electrification. In the midst of it all, a type 4 diesel No. D309 *Shamrock* heads the 8.15 a.m. Liverpool to London Euston past the site on 31 May 1963.

B. Brooksbank

'Jubilee' class No. 46149 *The Middlesex Regiment* shoots through Welton, between Weedon and Rugby, with the up 'Manxman' on a summer's day in 1952.

Les Hanson

The Leamington Line

The old, attractive, wooden platforms and main station buildings of Daventry between trains two years before closure, which occurred in August 1958.

Lens of Sutton

Daventry station down platform, which, unlike its counterpart on the up side, consisted of a simple waiting room and office. In the background the line curves off to Leamington.

Lens of Sutton

Braunston London Road station on 15 April 1962, some four years after the last passenger services used it in August 1958. Freight workings ceased in December 1963.

B. Brooksbank

Northampton to Bedford

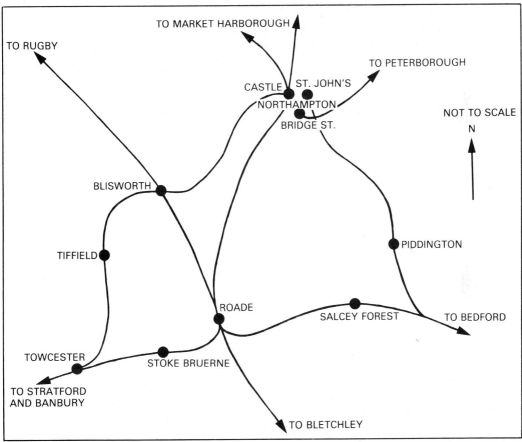

The location of Northampton St John's Street station in relation to the other stations in Northampton. Originally this station was designed to cater for the Bedford services but it lost its passenger status in July 1939, after which the track layout was altered so that trains could be diverted into Northampton Castle. Goods traffic survived for only two months longer. Also indicated on the map are the stations of Tiffield and Salcey Forest on the Shakespeare route, closed to passenger traffic in 1871 and 1893 respectively.

On a rather dank February day in 1962, the station-master waits to do his duty as the Bedford railmotor train headed by Derby class 2MT 2-6-2T No. 84005 draws into Piddington from Northampton Castle.

K.C.H. Fairey

Almost a month before closure, this view shows the station at Piddington at a deserted moment on 15 February 1962. The station attracted little custom because it was miles from any habitation. Note that this rural byway was double tracked, even though business on the line did not warrant it.

K.C.H. Fairey

The Bedford railmotor headed by locomotive No. 84005 passes Piddington signal-box and goods yard, at which point a short spur diverged to the left to a quarry.

K.C.H. Fairey

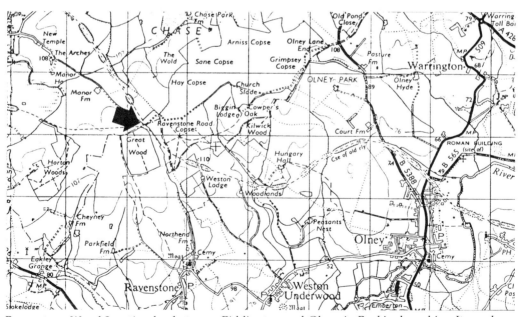

Ravenstone Wood Junction lay between Piddington and Olney in Buckinghamshire. It was here that the little-used Stoke Bruerne line met the Northampton Castle to Bedford line.

Northampton to Peterborough

The rather immaculate station at Northampton Bridge Street with a Wellingborough railmotor train just departing, headed by 2MT class 2-6-2T No. 41227.

K.C.H. Fairey

No trains present but obviously one is due as a number of passengers have gathered on the up platform in this view of Northampton Bridge Street taken on 9 August 1959.

Les Hanson

The Wellingborough railmotor headed by a 2MT class No. 41225 draws into the west end of Northampton Bridge Street station past the goods depot on 2 May 1964, which marked the last day of services.

K.C.H. Fairey

During a quiet spell on 4 July 1959, the photographer had a splendid opportunity to capture the wonderfully ornate design on the main station building at Northampton Bridge Street, created by John Livock in an Elizabethan style with two gables separated by stone balustrades, which in turn were set off by a simple platform awning supported by scroll brackets.

H.C. Casserley

On the last day of service, the railmotor service from Wellingborough, having just disgorged its passengers, awaits the right away from Northampton Bridge Street to Northampton Castle.

K.C.H. Fairey

Having just left Northampton Bridge Street station, the last afternoon railmotor service passes the signal-box of the same name on 2 May 1964. Note the big wheel in the signal cabin, which was for controlling the level-crossing gates.

K.C.H. Fairey

Arousing a considerable amount of interest is the 'Grafton Rail Tour', hauled by class 5MT No. 45139, which is seen here approaching the station at Northampton Bridge Street on 9 August 1959.

Les Hanson

Unlike the other stations on the Wellingborough line, Billing did not remain open until the end, having been closed on 6 October 1952, some twelve years before this view was taken; Stanier class 5MT 2-6-0 No. 42982 is seen on a Wellingborough to Northampton Bridge Street working on 23 April 1964.

K.C.H. Fairey

Super-power as B1 class No. 61204 draws past the signal cabin and into Castle Ashby station with a Northampton to Peterborough working on 20 May 1962.

K.C.H. Fairey

The rather attractive and well-kept diminutive waiting shelter at Castle Ashby on 2 May 1964, seen just prior to the arrival of the last train.

Les Hanson

A few days before the end of services, class 2MT No. 41225, leaking a bit, draws gently into Castle Ashby with a Northampton to Wellingborough railmotor on 30 April 1964.

K.C.H. Fairey

On a rather dreary day in April 1964, Ivatt class 2MT 2-6-2T No. 41227 drifts gently past the signal cabin and into the platform of Wellingborough London Road station.

K.C.H. Fairey

Wellingborough London Road on 1 May 1959 with an ex-LNER D16 No. 62597 at the head of the 9.54 a.m. cross-country service from Northampton to Peterborough.

K.C.H. Fairey

Fairburn class 4MT No. 42064 at Wellingborough London Road with a Peterborough to Northampton working on 25 April 1964.

K.C.H. Fairey

A fine overall view of the station complex that made up Wellingborough London Road station, where a 4F class No. 44215 is seen waiting for custom on a Peterborough to Northampton Castle working on 18 August 1962. In the background lies the curve to the Midland Road station.

Author's Collection

5MT Stanier class 2-6-0 No. 42970 rushes past Ditchford station with a Peterborough to Northampton Castle train on 30 April 1964, some forty years after passenger trains had ceased to call here. Facilities for goods remained a while longer, until 1950.

K.C.H. Fairey

Irthlingborough station, facing Northampton, on 29 June 1955.

R.M. Casserley

A mixed goods train for Peterborough rushes along between Irthlingborough and Ringstead and Addington on 2 June 1959 headed by B1 class No. 61295.

Author's Collection

Thrapston Bridge Street station on 2 May 1964 just two days before closure. On the right a train is about to depart for Peterborough.

Les Hanson

Another view of Thrapston Bridge Street station, this time looking towards Peterborough from the Northampton end of the station on 13 April 1959.

R.M. Casserley

The disused trackbed on the Northampton to Peterborough line near Thorpe station in 1971.

Author's Collection

A quiet moment at Barnwell station on the Northampton to Peterborough route, facing Northampton, on 22 April 1959.

R.M. Casserley

A couple of passengers head for the station on a dull day in 1964 as the photographer takes the opportunity to record a scene that was fast vanishing from the railway network: a country station like Barnwell with its level crossing, different-styled buildings and uneven platforms.

B. Brooksbank

Oundle station on 18 April 1964 as Stanier class 5 4-6-0 No. 44936 backs on to a few wagons before departing with a Northampton Castle to Peterborough East pick-up freight working.

K.C.H. Fairey

The Midland Main Line

Doncaster-built class 5MT No. 73073 is seen charging along south of Irchester station with a Leeds to London express on 23 June 1962.

Author's Collection

'Jubilee' class No. 45573 *Newfoundland* steadily climbs up Sharnbrook Bank with an up Manchester Central to London St Pancras express. Just above the tail end of the train, on the bridge, is the rather stylish booking hall for Irchester station.

2-6-2T class 2MT engine waits for custom in platform 2 of Wellingborough Midland Road station before departing for Northampton Castle.

K.C.H. Fairey

On 28 May 1959 tank-engine No. 84006 sits in platform 5 of Wellingborough Midland Road station with the 3.52 p.m. train to Higham Ferrers.

K.C.H. Fairey

An overall view of Wellingborough Midland Road station from the north end, with the Higham Ferrers railmotor set forming a Northampton to Kettering working on 29 June 1961.

K.C.H. Fairey

BR 2-10-0 9F class No. 92085 leans as it streaks round the curved platform 2 of Wellingborough Midland Road with a mineral train for Cricklewood.

Les Hanson

'Royal Scot' class *The Green Howards* No. 46133 rushes through the main up platform of Wellingborough Midland Road with the 12.04 p.m. ex-Manchester Piccadilly to London St Pancras on 20 April 1961.

K.C.H. Fairey

An immaculate 4-6-0 'Black 5' class No. 45156 *Ayrshire Yeomanry* prepares a train of coaches in Wellingborough carriage sidings, while a stopping train from Leicester to London St Pancras eases away from the station, on 31 May 1959.

K.C.H. Fairey

Ex-London Midland and Scottish Railway and formerly London and North Western Railway class 1P 0-4-4T No. 58091, built in 1881, stands in platform 5 at Wellingborough Midland Road station with two coaches which were to form an afternoon departure to Higham Ferrers on 2 October 1954.

K.C.H. Fairey

BR 9F class No. 92138 heads away from the Wellingborough Midland Road station complex with a mixed freight train for Nottingham on 1 August 1957.

Author's Collection

A splendid sight as 7P 'Jubilee' class *Bellerophon* draws effortlessly along through the massive network of tracks just north of Willingborough Midland Road station in January 1961 with a London St Pancras to Leeds express.

Author's Collection

2MT class 2-6-0 No. 78028 is seen here passing Wellingborough North signal cabin in a Leicester to Bedford local service in August 1958.

On a rather murky day in 1960 4F class 0-6-0 No. 44591 storms past Wellingborough engine shed with an express freight for Derby.

Super-power as 2P class No. 30536 and 7P 'Jubilee' class No. 45569 *Tasmania* head a London St Pancras to Glasgow express past Wellingborough engine depot and goods yard on a July evening in 1959.

Author's Collection

3F class 0-6-0 No. 43785 has been retired from duty after many years of service and is seen here in store at Wellingborough shed yard on 24 March 1957, awaiting her final journey to the breakers' yard.

Author's Collection

Due to engineering works, a Bradford to London St Pancras relief train, headed by Stanier class 5 4-6-0 No. 45285, is just crossing from the up slow to the up fast line near Finedon Road, Wellingborough.

Author's Collection

An up special train from Manchester Central to London St Pancras thunders along past the platformless station buildings of Finedon on 31 March 1964, twenty or so years after it closed on 2 December 1940.

K.C.H. Fairey

Ex-War Department locomotive No. 90888, complete with a snowplough, rushes past Finedon Station signal cabin with a train of mineral empties returning to York on 8 March 1963.

K.C.H. Fairey

On the same day, also at Finedon, class 2MT 2-6-2T No. 84005 is seen trundling along with its two coaches which formed the Northampton to Kettering local service.

K.C.H. Fairey

A modern 'Peak' type 4 diesel-electric D68 with a Leeds to London St Pancras express rushes past another long-abandoned station on the former Midland main line, namely Burton Latimer (formerly Isham and Burton Latimer), which saw its last passengers on 20 November 1950, though goods facilities still continued to be provided until the late 1960s.

B. Brooksbank

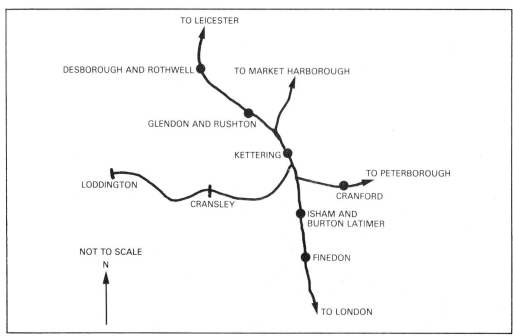

A plan of the short goods line that served Cransley and Loddington, diverging from the Midland main line at the south-western corner of Kettering station. This route was used for freight traffic only and never saw passengers.

On a foul, wet day in May 1959, 2MT class Ivatt 2-6-0 No. 46444 eases gently out of the east bay of
Kettering station with the 2.10 p.m. local service to Cambridge.

K.C.H. Fairey

Vintage motive power at Kettering shed on 7 August 1954 as ex-LNER class J36 No. 65390 basks in the sun with other more modern counterparts.

Author's Collection

'Jubilee' class No. 45626 *Seychelles* stands silently outside Kettering shed on 11 July 1964 after a day's duty. She was finally withdrawn in November 1965.

Author's Collection

Having just coaled up, 'Jubilee' class locomotive No. 45573 *Newfoundland* awaits her turn of duty in the siding alongside the coaling stage at Kettering shed.

Author's Collection

Class 3F 0-6-0 No. 43721 draws an engineers' train along the up slow line through Kettering station on 8 April 1958.

K.C.H. Fairey

On 29 March 1962, a rather immaculate Ivatt class 4MT 2-6-0 No. 43048 heads an up mixed freight through Kettering. Note the Gresley full-brake vehicle in the middle of the train.

K.C.H. Fairey

With a tremendous cloud of smoke, 4F class 0-6-0 No. 44103 skirts through the up fast platform at Kettering with a freight for Cricklewood on 8 April 1958.

K.C.H. Fairey

Super-power as Stanier class 5MT No. 44810 and 'Royal Scot' class No. 46103 *Royal Scots Fusilier* struggle as they depart from Kettering with a heavily-laden Bradford to London St Pancras express on 27 December 1958.

K.C.H. Fairey

'Royal Scot' class No. 46115 *Scots Guardsman* leans as it runs round the curve at the north end of Kettering station, with its train of new British Railways Mk 1 carriages which are forming a Manchester Piccadilly to London St Pancras express on 29 March 1962.

K.C.H. Fairey

4P class three-cylinder compound 0-6-0 No. 41059, on a sunny autumn afternoon in 1953, drifts along lazily near Glendon Junction with a Kettering to Leicester local service.

M. Marston

DESBOROUGH
& ROTHWELL

An example of one of the totem signs at Desborough and Rothwell station. These signs were designed to be fixed to lamp-posts. Note the inclusion of Rothwell in smaller letters, which was done because this village was a mile away from the station, which was situated in the centre of Desborough.

Author's Collection

Kettering Quarries

Kettering Furnaces No. 2, with a fully-laden train of ore and two oil drums in the wagon nearest the
locomotive, sets off for the plant in the background on 14 April 1959.

R.M. Casserley

On one of the Kettering Quarry railway sidings, the small but powerful industrial tank-engine *Kettering Furnaces No. 8* awaits its turn of duty on 18 July 1958.

R.M. Casserley

An interesting picture as *Kettering Furnaces No. 2* draws its laden train along the staithes at Kettering Works on 14 April 1959.

R.M. Casserley

With H.C. Casserley on the footplate, the diminutive locomotive *Kettering Furnaces No. 2* has come to the end of the line with its train. At this point minerals were collected from standard gauge railway wagons that had come from the main line.

R.M. Casserley

One of the many mineral wagons that belonged to the Kettering Furnaces Company seen here on 14 April 1959.

H.C. Casserley

Wellingborough to Higham Ferrers

Having just disgorged a number of passengers on 28 May 1959, No. 84006 with its two-coach railmotor set waits to depart from Rushden on a Higham Ferrers to Wellingborough Midland Road train.

K.C.H. Fairey

Rushden station as photographed from the 3.52 p.m. Wellingborough Midland Road to Higham Ferrers service on 28 May 1959.

K.C.H. Fairey

A rather unusual arrival at Rushden as the LCGB's Bedford group charter, comprising a variety of brake-vans hauled by locomotive No. 78028, draws into the platform on 3 July 1965.

K.C.H. Fairey

Everything looks so immaculate and pristine considering it is the last day of passenger services on the Higham Ferrers branch. Here Derby-designed class 2MT 2-6-2T No. 84007 waits to depart from Rushden with the penultimate service to Wellingborough Midland Road on 13 June 1959.

Les Hanson

A small crowd has turned out to witness the final departure to Wellingborough from Higham Ferrers on 13 June 1959, which was propelled by locomotive No. 84007 and driven from the leading end of both the carriages it was sandwiched between.

Les Hanson

Higham Ferrers station on 28 May 1959 with engine No. 84006 and the railmotor set having just arrived with the 3.52 p.m. service from Wellingborough Midland Road.

K.C.H. Fairey

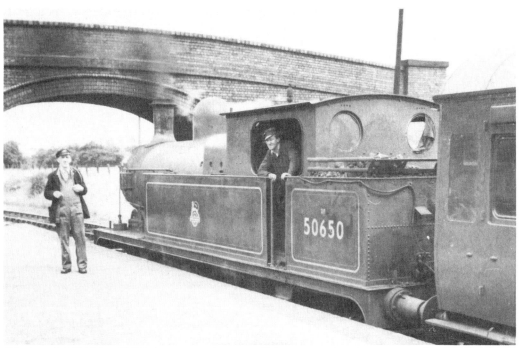

2P class 2-4-2T No. 50650 in pretty clean condition poses for the camera along with driver W. Fairey and fireman S. Abbott at Higham Ferrers station on 6 August 1956.

K.C.H. Fairey

Higham Ferrers on 13 June 1959, the last day of service, with a train from Wellingborough Midland Road sitting in the platform waiting for custom for the return journey. Note the ornamental lamps and posts which dated back to the construction of the line.

Les Hanson

A last look at the lovely station building of Higham Ferrers taken from the train before the last ever departure to Wellingborough Midland Road on 13 June 1959.

Les Hanson

The trackwork is still in good condition but, alas, the platform (which has been fenced off) and the station buildings are beginning to show signs of decay in this photograph, which recorded the arrival of the novel brake-van special at Higham Ferrers on 3 July 1965.

K.C.H. Fairey

Class 2MT 2-6-2T No. 84006 is seen standing at Higham Ferrers on 28 May 1959 waiting for custom.

K.C.H. Fairey

The rather elaborate goods facilities at Higham Ferrers, on 28 May 1959.

K.C.H. Fairey

The Varsity Line

'Jubliee' class No. 45660 *Rooke* draws an iron ore tripper through the disused Cranford station on 12 May 1965.

K.C.H. Fairey

On 19 February 1958 Derby-built class 2MT 2-6-0 No. 78021 heads along towards Twywell with a Ketting local service from Cambridge.

K.C.H. Fairey

'Jubilee' class No. 45660 *Rooke* waits by its train as a heavy lorry is busy loading it with ore from the dock at Twywell on 12 May 1965.

K.C.H. Fairey

Shunting manoeuvres at Twywell station, which lost its passenger services on 30 July 1951, eight years before the end of the Kettering to Cambridge local trains.

K.C.H. Fairey

A rather nice view of Thrapston Midland Road station taken from the 2.10 p.m. Kettering to Cambridge train as it draws to a halt on 21 May 1959.

K.C.H. Fairey

4P class No. 42350 stands at Thrapston Midland Road station with a heavy complement of coaches while working the 'Fernie Rail Tour' in August 1962.

Colour Rail

Industrial locomotive *Sir Berkeley* stands idle on one of the Cranford Ironstone Company's sidings on 18 July 1958.

R.M. Casserley

Another view of *Sir Berkeley*, this time shunting some iron ore tipplers at the Cranford Ironstone Company's sidings complex.

R.M. Casserley

The former Raunds station and goods yard two years after closure, on 16 April 1961. Note the concrete sleepered track, which was laid only a year or so before the cessation of passenger services on the Kettering to Cambridge line.

K.C.H. Fairey

Cranford, another of the Cranford Ironstone Company's engines, prepares to run round its train of empty iron ore tipplers at the complex's reception sidings.

R.M. Casserley

The Corby Route

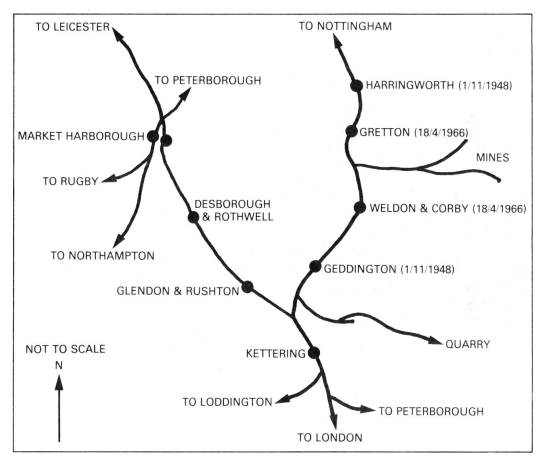

Map showing stations on the Corby route and their dates of closure to passenger and goods traffic. The line to Corby was reopened for a trial period on 1 May 1987 following pressure brought to bear on the local authorities and British Rail by growing industrial interests in the town. The experiment was so successful that electrification is now planned as far as Corby. The line has always generated much freight traffic.

One of the many industrial tank engines that worked on the Steward and Lloyds Steelworks railway at Corby, No. 34 *Calettwr* is seen standing outside the complex's depot on 22 April 1959.

H.C. Casserley

Rugby to Peterborough

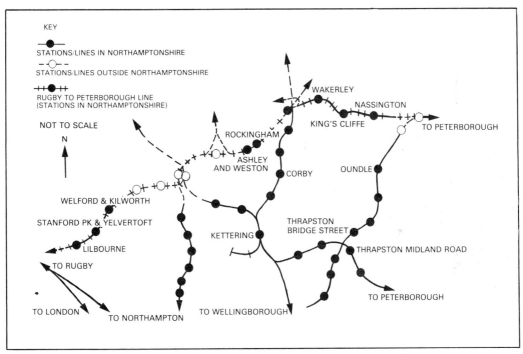

KEY

STATIONS/LINES IN NORTHAMPTONSHIRE

STATIONS/LINES OUTSIDE NORTHAMPTONSHIRE

RUGBY TO PETERBOROUGH LINE
(STATIONS IN NORTHAMPTONSHIRE)

NOT TO SCALE

N

WAKERLEY

NASSINGTON

KING'S CLIFFE

ROCKINGHAM

ASHLEY
AND WESTON

CORBY

OUNDLE

TO PETERBOROUGH

WELFORD & KILWORTH

STANFORD PK & YELVERTOFT

LILBOURNE

KETTERING

THRAPSTON
BRIDGE STREET

THRAPSTON MIDLAND ROAD

TO RUGBY

TO LONDON

TO NORTHAMPTON

TO WELLINGBOROUGH

TO PETERBOROUGH

Map of the meandering Rugby to Peterborough line which passed in and out of the county of
Northamptonshire three times along its route.

Welford and Kilworth station on 10 April 1965, facing Market Harborough. Note the array of new-looking British Railways square enamel signs and totems on the platform lamp-posts.

R.M. Casserley

A fine view of the signal cabin and waiting shelter at Rockingham station, further along the line between Market Harborough and Seaton. The shelter was in stark contrast to the massive building on the Rugby platform side.

Les Hanson

The level-crossing gates at Rockingham are here seen being manually closed to allow the Peterborough to Rugby pick-up goods to pass, on 23 April 1959.

H.C. Casserley

Northampton Castle

Doncaster-designed class 5MT No. 73070, introduced in 1951, trundles through the centre road at Northampton Castle with a freight for Willesden on 2 May 1964. This class of engine had a very short life span of just over fourteen years.

K.C.H. Fairey

'Prince Coronation' class 4-6-2 *Duchess of Atholl*, much to the delight of the spotter, heads past the junction to Blisworth with the down 'Royal Scot' on 23 July 1950.

Les Hanson

This time from the Blisworth route to Northampton Castle, another member of the 'Prince Coronation' class, No. 46227 *Duchess of Devonshire*, heads a 'Royal Scot' on 30 June 1951.

Les Hanson

'Jubilee' class No. 45672 *Anson* draws slowly past No. 2 signal cabin towards Northampton Castle with an up freight for Bletchley on 2 May 1964.

K.C.H. Fairey

4P class 4-4-0 three-cylinder compound No. 40937 simmers gently as she rests on the centre stabling road between platforms 5 and 6 of Northampton Castle.

H.C. Casserley

B1 class No. 61095, complete with an adapted tender, stands silently in the Peterborough bay platform with an early evening service on 31 July 1957.

Les Hanson

Northampton Castle station on 4 July 1959 with No. 84007 about to depart with its two-coach motor train for Wellingborough. Note the diesel railcar in the platform on the right.

R.M. Casserley

A sad scene at Northampton Castle on 2 May 1964 as the last trains to Peterborough and Wellingborough stand on the left and right respectively.

K.C.H. Fairey

After the departure of the Peterborough train, an Ivatt class 2MT 2-6-2T takes on water before making the final journey to Wellingborough Midland Road on 2 May 1964.

K.C.H. Fairey

On 5 March 1962 class 5MT No. 45113 draws into one of the south bays at Northampton Castle with a train from Peterborough.

K.C.H. Fairey

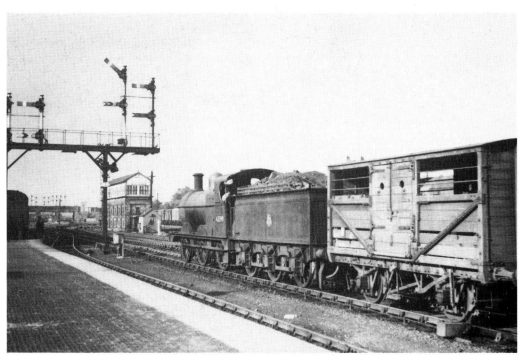

Having just got the right away from Northampton Castle, a class 3F 0-6-0 No. 43399 prepares to head off for Rugby with a train of vintage cattle-wagons on 14 September 1957.

Les Hanson

Super-power as class 7MT 4-6-2 *Iron Duke* blows off in a violent fashion as it draws along towards Northampton Castle on 19 May 1964 with a rake of coal wagons from Toton.

Les Hanson

All change at Northampton Castle, which by the time this picture was taken on 27 March 1965 had seen complete electrification and the construction of a new station, though this seems to be still unfinished judging by the bare canopy supports. This particular day also saw the appearance of a steam locomotive that was a stranger to Midland Region territory, namely No. 7029 *Clun Castle*, seen here at the head of an Ian Allan rail tour.

Author's Collection

The exterior of Northampton Castle on 19 February 1966, by this time the only station in the town, showing the imposing building that formed the approach to it. Note the futile exhibition being held in an attempt to woo passengers back to using the railways instead of the roads. What a pity this had not been held a few years earlier, before the end of the Wellingborough, Peterborough and Blisworth services.

Les Hanson

Northampton Castle on 2 January 1960 with 4P class 4-4-0 three-cylinder compound No. 41218 waiting to head off, bunker first, with a train to Market Harborough on the last day of service.

Les Hanson

On 4 July 1959, amid a mixture of locomotives and rolling stock, No. HE/96(645) *Saxon* stands at rest in one of the sidings at Northampton Gasworks.

H.C. Casserley

121

Northampton to the Midland

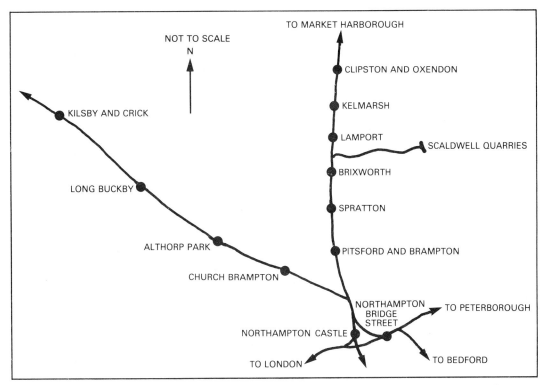

Map of the lines to the north-west of Northampton Castle station. Note the locations of Long Buckby, and Kilsby and Crick stations on the line to Rugby.

Pitsford and Brampton, the first stop after Northampton on the Market Harborough route, seen shortly after its closure on 5 June 1950.

Lens of Sutton

The derelict remains of Spratton station, which closed in 1949, just prior to the era covered in this book.

Lens of Sutton

An overall view of Brixworth station and goods yard on 1 May 1965, some five years after closure. While the station had closed, the line continued to see the odd flurry of traffic from Scaldwell Quarries.

B. Brooksbank

Inside the Scaldwell Quarries complex, showing the area known as the transhipment stage on 14 April 1959. Here the extracted mineral, which had been hauled along on a narrow-gauge line, was tipped into standard-gauge wagons which were shunted to the main line, where a further exchange took place before the freight could set off on its destination.

H.C. Casserley

Outside the locomotive depot at Scaldwell Quarries stand a couple of the complex's industrial locomotives. The one in the foreground, by the coaling stage, is in the process of being reassembled, while the engine behind is preparing for its turn of duty.

H.C. Casserley

The rather grey-looking station buildings at Lamport, devoid of all fixtures and fittings, are in a remarkably good state considering they have been out of use for four years.

Lens of Sutton

A sketch of what was known as a 'Hawkseye' station nameboard and oil-lamp at Lamport in 1958.
Author's Collection

On 11 April 1964, 'Jubilee' class No. 45556 *Nova Scotia* trundles along past Lamport with an up coal train from Leicester to Northampton Castle.

M. Mitchell

One of the original LMS station nameboards at Kelmarsh in 1960 just before the station closed.

Author's Collection

Demolition in earnest at Kelmarsh as the platforms are removed and the blocks stacked up ready for taking away and reusing for patching up other stations.

Lens of Sutton

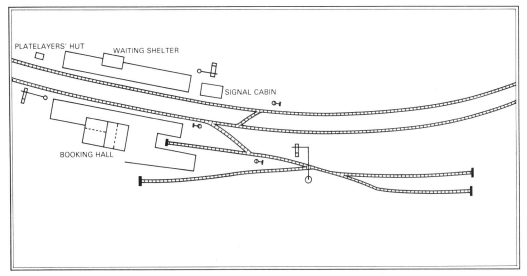

Plan of the station and track layout at Kelmarsh.

Author's Collection

The signal cabin at Clipston and Oxendon which was located by the entrance to the station's goods yard.

Lens of Sutton

The main station buildings at Clipston and Oxendon just after closure to passenger services on 4 January 1960.

Lens of Sutton

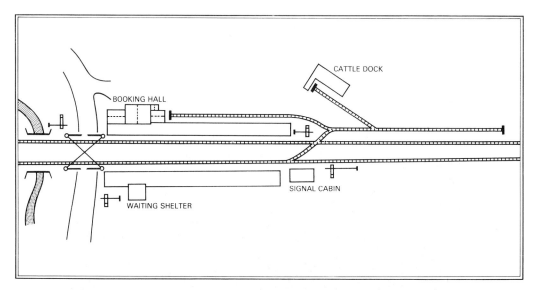

The track and station layout at Clipston and Oxendon at the time of closure in 1960.

Author's Collection

On the rails to Rugby

As the old station at Church Brampton, which closed on 18 May 1951, disappears beneath the cutting banks and the builders' rubble, the electrification masts are taking over, standing like proud sentinels.

Lens of Sutton

A photograph of the former station at Althorp Park as it sadly undergoes demolition two years after closure, which took place on 13 June 1960.

From a photocopy supplied by *Northamptonshire Chronicle and Echo*

Dates of Closure of Northamptonshire Stations

	To Passengers	To Goods
GREAT CENTRAL MAIN LINE		
Brackley Central	3 Sept 1966	14 June 1965
Helmdon for Sulgrave	4 March 1963	2 Nov 1964
Culworth	29 Sept 1958	29 Sept 1958
Woodford Halse	3 Sept 1966	5 April 1965
Charwelton	4 March 1963	4 March 1963
GREAT CENTRAL WOODFORD LINK		
Eydon Road Halt	2 April 1956	----------
Chacombe Road Halt	6 Feb 1956	----------
THE VERNEY JUNCTION TO BANBURY LINE		
Fulwell and Westbury	2 Jan 1961	2 Dec 1963
Farthinghoe	3 Nov 1952	2 Dec 1963
NORTHAMPTON AND BANBURY JUNCTION RAILWAY		
Helmdon Village	2 July 1951	29 Oct 1951
Wappenham	2 July 1951	29 Oct 1951
THE SHAKESPEARE ROUTE		
Byfield	7 April 1952	4 May 1964
Morton Pinkney	7 April 1952	7 April 1952
Blakesley	7 April 1952	3 Sept 1962
Towcester	7 April 1952	3 Feb 1964
Tiffield	1 March 1871	----------
Stoke Bruerne	31 March 1893	2 June 1952
Salcey Forest	31 March 1893	1 July 1908
THE WEST COAST MAIN LINE		
Roade	7 Sept 1964	7 Sept 1964
Blisworth SMJR	7 April 1952	6 July 1964
Blisworth LNWR	4 Jan 1960	6 July 1964
Weedon	15 Sept 1958	----------
Welton	7 July 1958	----------
THE LEAMINGTON LINE		
Daventry	15 Sept 1958	2 Dec 1963
Braunston London Road	15 Sept 1958	2 Dec 1963

	To Passengers	To Goods

NORTHAMPTON TO BEDFORD

Northampton St John's Street	3 July 1939	3 July 1939
Piddington	5 March 1962	5 March 1962

NORTHAMPTON TO PETERBOROUGH

Northampton Bridge Street	4 May 1964	----------
Billing	6 Oct 1952	1 June 1964
Castle Ashby	4 May 1964	1 Feb 1965
Wellingborough London Road	4 May 1964	7 Nov 1966
Ditchford	1 Nov 1924	15 May 1950
Ringstead and Addington	4 May 1964	2 March 1964
Thrapston Bridge Street	4 May 1964	7 June 1965
Thorpe	4 May 1964	4 May 1964
Barnwell	4 May 1964	4 May 1964
Oundle	4 May 1964	6 June 1972

THE MIDLAND MAIN LINE

Irchester	7 March 1960	4 Jan 1965
Wellingborough Midland Road	----------	----------
Finedon	2 Dec 1940	6 July 1964
Isham and Burton Latimer	2 Nov 1950	6 July 1964
Kettering	----------	----------
Glendon and Rushton	4 Jan 1960	6 July 1964
Desborough and Rothwell	1 Jan 1968	1 Jan 1968

THE HIGHAM FERRERS BRANCH

Rushden	15 June 1959	1 Sept 1969
Higham Ferrers	15 June 1959	3 Feb 1969

THE VARSITY LINE

Cranford	2 April 1956	6 Nov 1961
Twywell	30 Jan 1951	30 July 1951
Thrapston Midland Road	15 June 1959	28 Oct 1963
Raunds	15 June 1959	28 Oct 1963

THE CORBY ROUTE

Geddington	1 Nov 1948	1 Nov 1948
Weldon and Corby	18 April 1966 (reopened 1987)	----------
Gretton	18 April 1966	----------
Harringworth	1 Nov 1948	1 Nov 1948

RUGBY TO PETERBOROUGH

Lilbourne	6 June 1966	----------
Stanford Park and Yelvertoft	6 June 1966	6 July 1964
Welford and Kilworth	6 June 1966	6 July 1964
Ashley and Weston	18 June 1951	8 July 1964
Rockingham	6 June 1966	6 April 1964
Wakerley and Barrowden	6 June 1966	28 Dec 1964
King's Cliffe	6 June 1966	3 June 1966
Nassington	1 July 1957	3 Aug 1957

	To Passengers	To Goods

NORTHAMPTON TO MARKET HARBOROUGH

Station	To Passengers	To Goods
Northampton Castle	----------	----------
Pitsford and Brampton	5 June 1950	5 June 1950
Spratton	23 May 1949	23 May 1949
Brixworth	4 Jan 1960	4 Jan 1960
Lamport	4 Jan 1960	4 Jan 1960
Kelmarsh	4 Jan 1960	4 Jan 1960
Clipston and Oxendon	4 Jan 1960	4 Jan 1960

NORTHAMPTON TO RUGBY

Station	To Passengers	To Goods
Church Brampton	18 May 1931	----------
Althorp Park	13 June 1960	----------
Long Buckby	----------	6 July 1964
Kilsby and Crick	1 Feb 1960	6 July 1964